The Happy Lines Family
Halloween Dinosaur
Coloring and Activity Book

Copyright © 2023 C. & L. & H. Lopez Espina

Published by The Little Book Farmers Happy Lines Family

Published in the United States of America

All rights reserved. No part of this publication can be reproduced, copied, transmitted, stored, or recorded in any manner whatsoever without written permission from the copyright owners. Commercial resale in any form is strictly prohibited.

To request permission, contact Little Book Farmers/ *The Happy Lines Family* at:

https://littlebookfarmers.com/contact-us/

Written and Edited by: C. & L. & H. Lopez Espina
Illustrated by: L. Lopez Espina

ISBN: 978-1-962850-05-6

My Halloween Dinosaur Book

This book belongs to:

Date: _____

Triceratops

Triceratops (pronounced try-se-ra-tops), meaning "three-horned face," is one of the most well-known and loved dinosaurs. They lived in North America and were about the size of an elephant.

Dino-Halloween!

Happy Halloween

Ankylosaurus

Ankylosaurus (pronounced ank-o-low-so-rus) was a 20-foot herbivore (plant eater), covered in an armor of plates and spikes, with a big, strong-clubbed tail to defend itself.

The Halloween Folding Game Part 1

The **Halloween Folding Game** is a fun two-to-three player game. You will need a sheet of paper and a pen or pencil. You can use crayons or colored pencils too.

How to play:

1. Fold a piece of paper into three equal sections just like you would fold a letter into an envelope. Number each folded segment: 1. for the head, 2. for the neck and body, and 3. for the legs and feet.

2. **The first player** draws the head of the Halloween creature on fold 1. When finished, fold the paper inward under segment three. Next, draw two small marks on segment 2. to show where the neck and body will continue. Make sure no one can see your drawing!

3. **The next player** draws the neck and body on segment 2. using the marks as a starting point. Then turn the paper over to section 3. and mark where the legs and feet begin. Pass it to the next player without letting anyone see what has been drawn.

4. **The last player** draws the legs and feet on segment 3. Then all together open up the folded paper to reveal a hilarious Halloween creature!

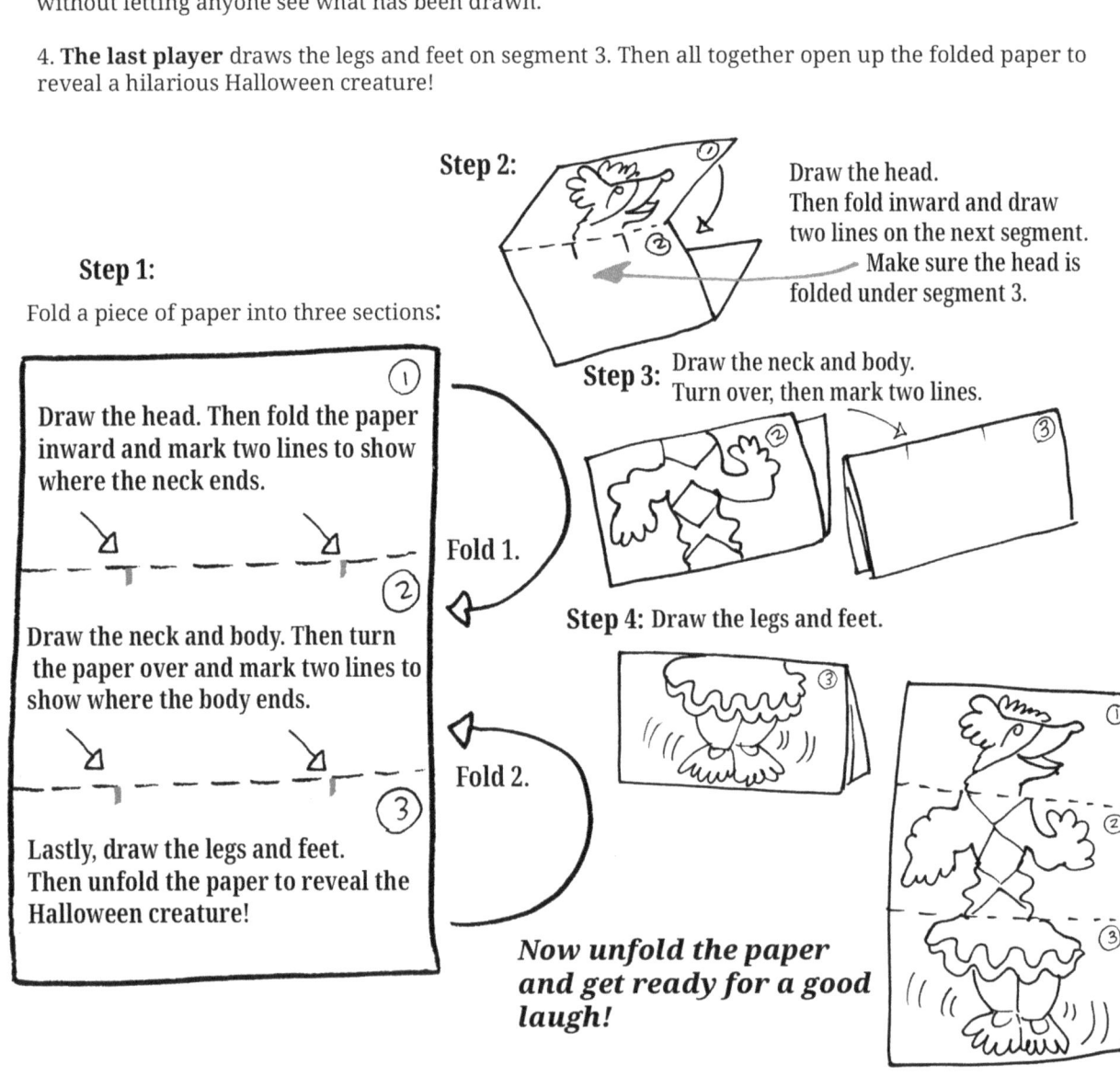

1.

2.

3.

1.

2.

3.

1.

2.

3.

1.

2.

3.

The Halloween Folding Game Part 2:
The Halloween Mix-Match Game

Once you have played **The Halloween Folding Game Part 1**, you can try **The Halloween Mix-Match Game**. You will need to have three or more completed Halloween creatures, and a pair of scissors.

1. Cut along each of the folds.

2. Lay all the pieces face down on a large surface (table, floor, etc.) and mix them up.

3. Each player chooses three pieces to begin making new creatures. But, this time, they may all turn out to be heads or feet. You can keep playing until someone gets a complete creature.

4. You can also have lots of fun putting together different combinations to find the funniest creatures of all.

5. Use your imagination. Don't forget that you can always invent new games. The possibilities are endless!

You can save all of your drawings in an envelope to play later.
The more drawings you save up, the funnier the game will become!

A little history about Tic-Tac-Toe:

Versions of the game Tic-Tac-Toe can be traced back to ancient times.

The Egyptians played a version with rocks and shells.

The Romans used pebbles in a game called, "Terni Lapilli," meaning three-pebbles-at-a-time.

An Native American version of the game is called, "Picaria".

In China, Tic-Tac-Toe is called "Jǐng Zì Qí" or "Quān Quān Chā Chā".

"Marupeke" is the Japanese name for Tic-Tac-Toe.

In the United Kingdom, the Republic of Ireland, New Zealand, Australia, parts of Africa, and India, Tic-Tac-Toe is known as "Noughts/Naughts and Crosses".

In Spanish-speaking countries, it's known as, "Tres en Raya," and "Totito".

You can do some research on your own to find out more, and to learn how to play fun versions of the game from around the world and long ago.

Dinosaur Tic-Tac-Toe

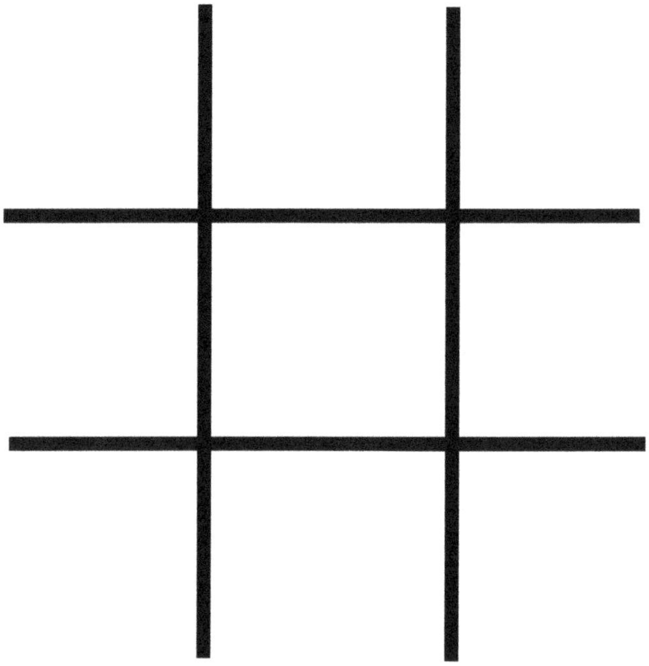

Dinosaur Tic-Tac-Toe comes from the two-player game called Tic-Tac-Toe.

Instructions:

1. Color the page however you like.
2. Carefully cut out the pieces.
3. You can laminate the pieces with packing tape to make them last longer.
4. Decorate an envelope to store the game board and pieces. If you don't have one, you can make one by stapling, or taping two pieces of paper together.

How to play:

1. Each player gets a set of five like pieces.
2. The youngest player goes first, placing one of their pieces on any square.
3. Each person gets one turn at a time until someone wins by getting three pieces in a row.
4. In some cases, no one gets three in a row. That's called a draw. Have fun!

Allosaurus Jimmadseni

Allosaurus Jimmadseni (pronounced al-low-so-rus jih-mad-se-ni) is a **theropod** (meat-eating dinosaur) from the **Allosaur family**, discovered at **Dinosaur National Monument** in Utah. They were an **apex predator** (which means they were at the top of the food chain; in other words, no animal would have dared to try and eat them.

Draw a face on the pumpkin

Name your pumpkin:

_____

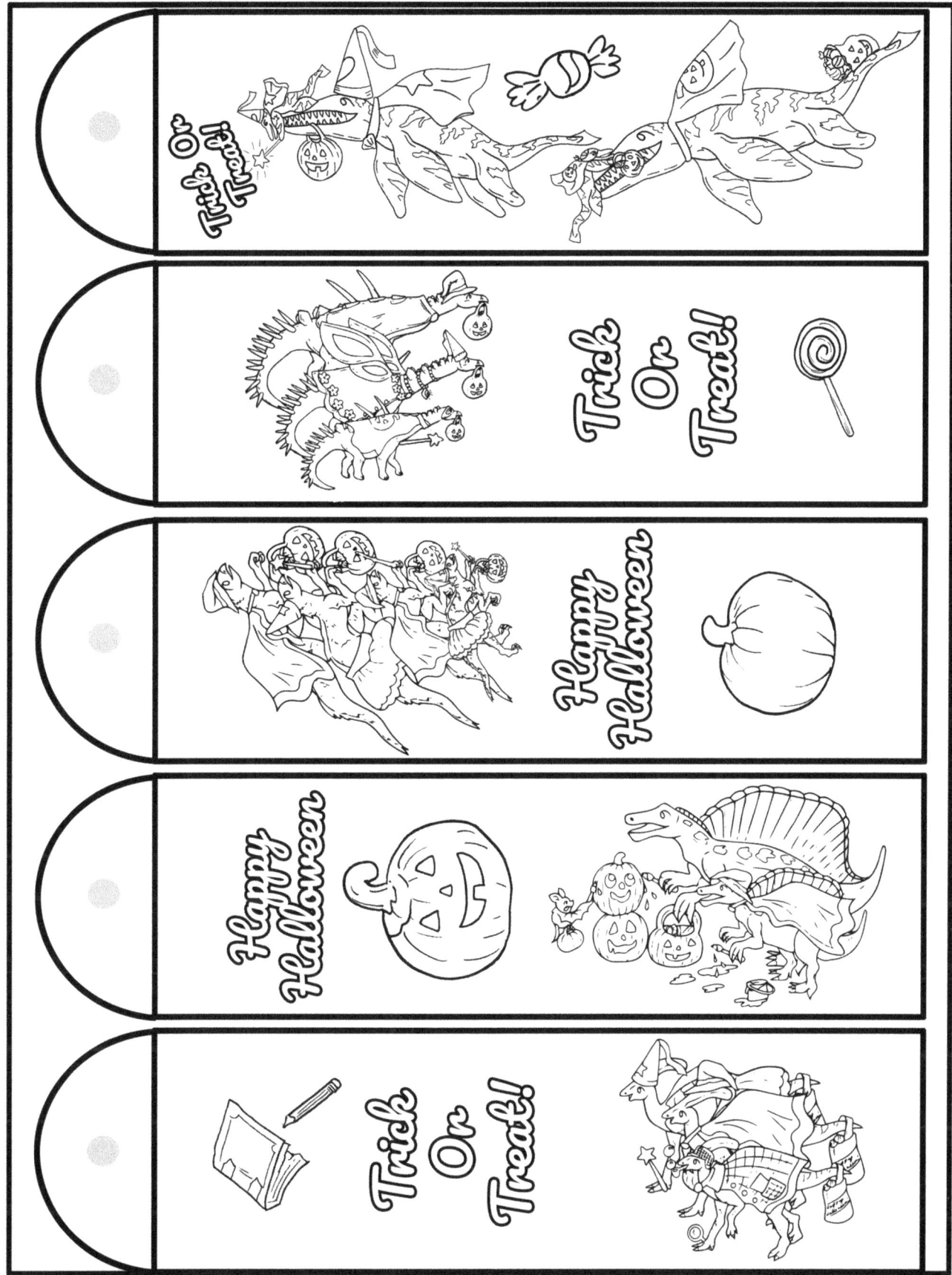

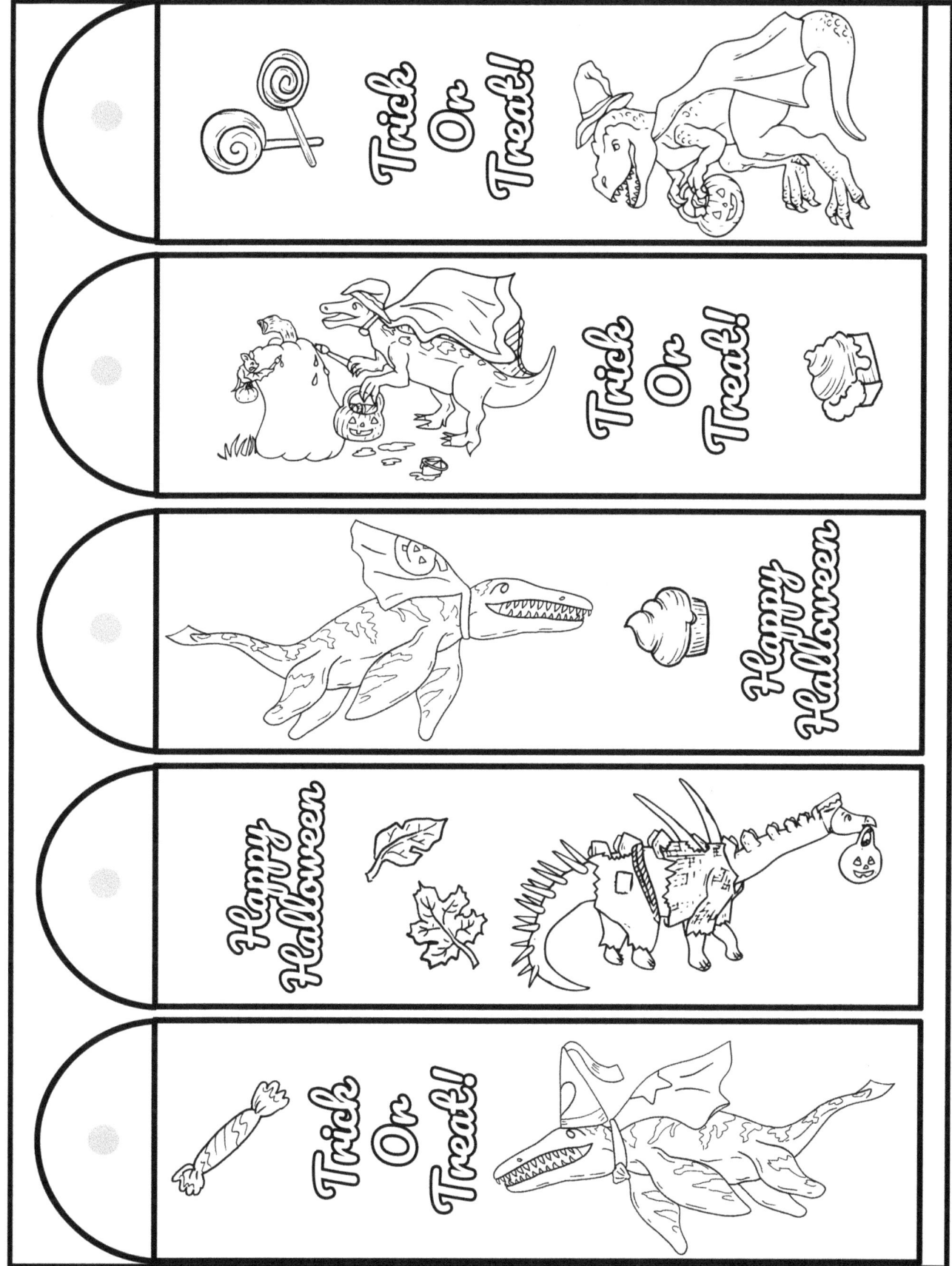

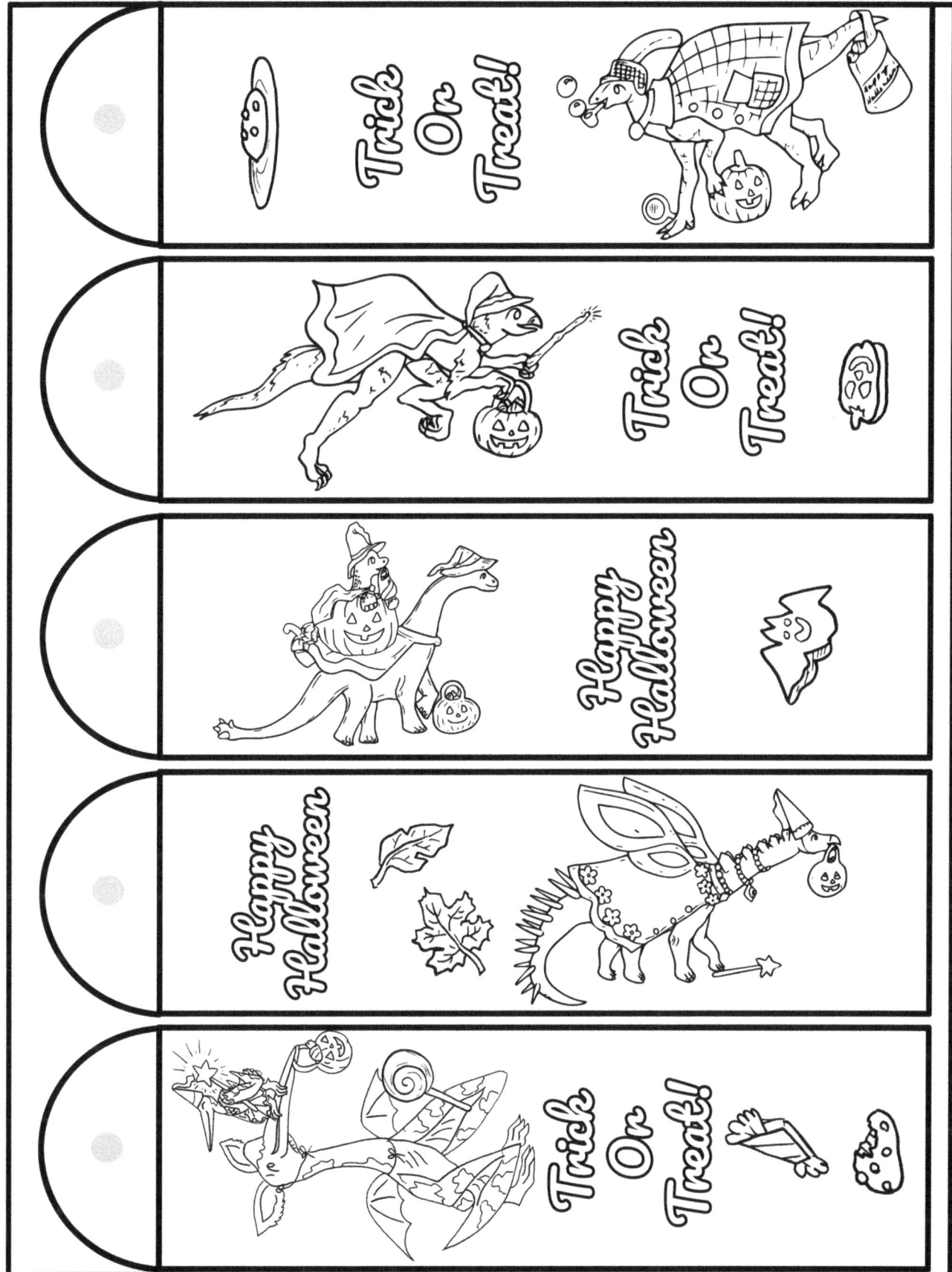

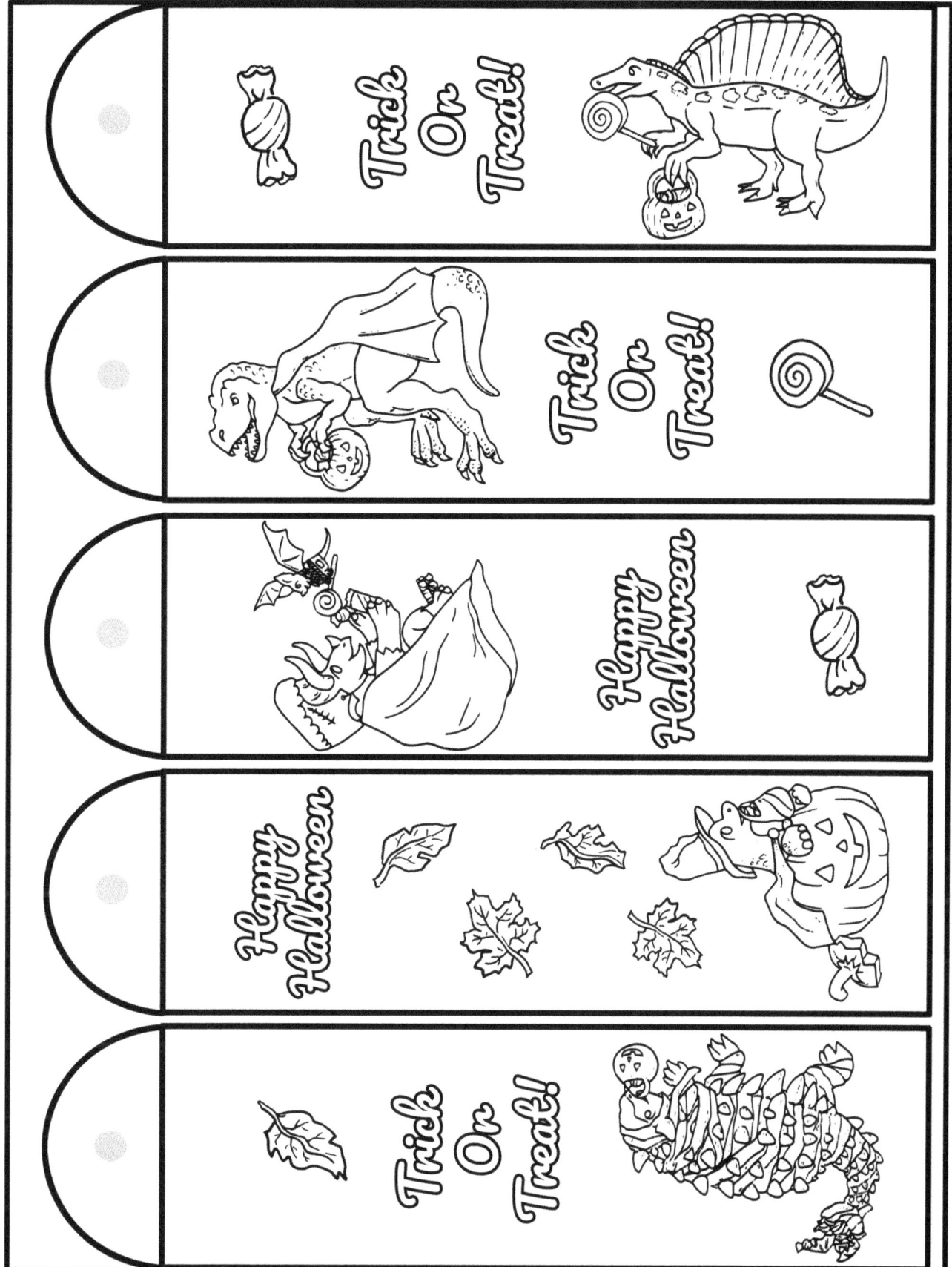

Hypsilophodon

Hypsilophodon (pronounced hip-so-lof-a-don) was a small **bipedal** dinosaur, which means they walked on two legs; discovered in England. They weighed about 40–50 pounds, similar to the weight of a nine-year-old child, and were about 4-6 feet long. They were known to be **herbivores** (plant eaters), but most likely they were **omnivores**, which means that they ate both plants and animals like many humans do. Feathered fossil imprints have been found in similar species. Do you think **Hypsilophodon** had feathers?

Prehistoric Halloween Word Search

Tip: Search row by row, up, down, backward, and diagonally (means across). Never give up, you will find them all!

D	I	N	O	S	A	U	R	L	A	M	S
B	I	G	Z	L	O	V	E	B	O	O	T
H	F	O	O	T	P	R	I	N	T	O	A
A	A	Z	H	O	S	T	O	M	P	N	R
P	Q	L	X	F	O	S	S	I	L	X	S
P	U	C	L	O	L	L	I	P	O	P	W
Y	G	W	O	O	P	U	M	P	K	I	N
H	E	A	R	D	W	Y	Q	D	W	E	E
W	O	N	D	E	R	E	G	I	A	N	T
L	O	N	G	A	G	O	E	G	F	U	N
Y	U	M	M	Y	Q	C	A	N	D	Y	W
T	R	I	C	K	O	R	T	R	E	A	T

1. Halloween
2. Candy
3. Trick Or Treat
4. Dinosaur
5. Happy
6. Big
7. Giant
8. Long Ago
9. Stars
10. Moon
11. Fun
12. Foot Print
13. Boo
14. Lollipop
15. Heard
16. Stomp
17. Yummy
18. Candy
19. Pumpkin
20. Fossil
21. Dig

Oviraptor

Oviraptors were feathered dinosaurs, and **doting parents**, despite their name, meaning **"egg thief"**. An oviraptor fossil was discovered in Mongolia caring for her eggs. It took time to find out that the eggs were not stolen, but in fact, her very own brood! Oviraptors were approximately five feet long.

Pin the Tail on Pumpkin Oviraptor

Instructions:

1. Color in Pumpkin Oviraptor and all 5 tails.

2. Cut out Pumpkin Oviraptor and each of the 5 numbered tails. Cut along the dotted lines.

3. You can laminate Pumpkin Oviraptor and all the tails in a laminator, or with packing tape to make them last longer.

4. You can decorate an envelope to save all your playing pieces for later. If you don't have an envelope, you can make one by stapling, or taping two pieces of paper together.

How to play:

Pin the Tail on Pumpkin Oviraptor is a game you can play by yourself or with up to 4 other people.

You can play in two ways: on a tabletop or on a wall. To play on a wall, you will need tape or pins. To play on a tabletop, you won't need any tape or pins.

1. Set Pumpkin Oviraptor on a tabletop or Pin or tape Pumpkin Oviraptor onto a wall or pin board.

2. Give each player a tail, and a piece of tape to each person if you are playing on a wall so they can attach their tail to Pumpkin Oviraptor.

3. The youngest player goes first. Either blindfold the player or have them squeeze their eyes shut tightly.

4. Each player takes a turn placing their tail where they think it should go.

5. Have fun playing!

Pin the Tail on Pumpkin Oviraptor Examples:

These are some of the funny possibilities that can happen when playing:

Remove page, then cut along the dotted lines.

Pin the Tail on Pumpkin Oviraptor:

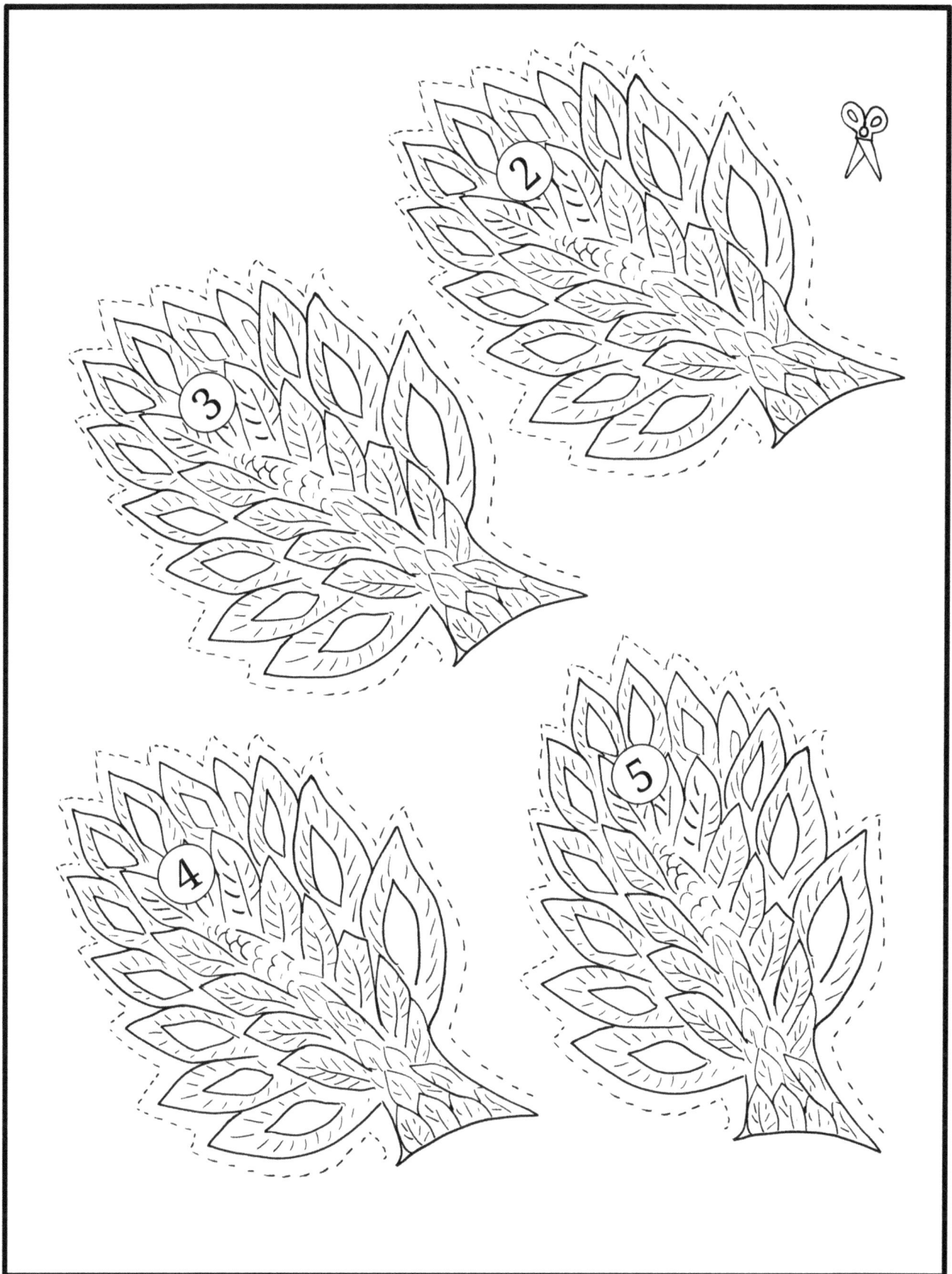

Color in the Pumpkin Oviraptor playing page. Then cut along the dotted line to remove page.

Parasaurolophus

Parasaurolophus (pronounced pear-a-suh-ra-la-fus), also called **Parasaur** and nicknamed **the trombone dinosaur**, lived in western North America. They were 33-foot-long **herbivores** (plant eaters), about the size of two giraffes. Their large head crests were used to make loud trumpeting sounds. Can you imagine what they sounded like? Now you can try to make your best Parasaurolophus sound. Just be careful not to try it in a library!

Halloween Story Game: Dinosaur Amusement Park!

Finish the story however you like, and draw a picture to go with it!

We were going to a dinosaur amusement park when suddenly the dinosaur statues began to move and...

Halloween Story Game: Dinosaur Amusement Park!

You can continue your story here:

Make a Halloween Sandwich for your Dinosaur friend.

Ingredients:
_____
_____
_____
_____

Liopleurodon

Liopleurodon (pronounced lie-oh-plur-a-don): Do you know who this is? It's the mighty Liopleurodon! A kind of **plesiosaur** (which is a type of marine reptile,) not to be confused with a dinosaur, although they lived during the same time. They were about 16–33 feet long (roughly the size of two giraffes).

Halloween Tic-Tac-Toe

You can use pennies and nickles, or two kinds of candy, or you can cut out the pumpkin cookie and cupcake playing pieces from this page, and have fun!

Happy Halloween!

Have a Bright & Happy Halloween!

Word Fill-In Game:
The Prehistoric Halloween Buffet

Instructions: You can play this word game with family, friends, or by yourself. First fill in the numbered blank spaces in the **Prehistoric Halloween Fill-In Word** page with the type of word it asks you for, but **don't** look at the story page until you finish.

Next fill in the numbered blank spaces on the **The Prehistoric Halloween Buffet Menu** story page with the words from your word fill-in list. Read it out loud and have lots of fun.

A **NOUN** is a word that names everything, a person, a place, or a thing. From the smallest to the biggest things that exist, from a planet to a pencil, from a microbe to a galaxy, a noun is simply the names of everything and anything real or imaginary.

A **VERB** is a word that describes an action. Anything that a noun is doing is a verb.
For example: run, jump, dance, sing, laugh, yell, read, sleep, eat, blink. Even to think or to stand still is an action!

An **ADJECTIVE** is a word that describes a noun. A noun can be: big, small, fuzzy, happy, energetic, grumpy, sweet, blue, messy, smooth, bumpy, beautiful, sour, smart, strange, funny, silly. Adjetives describe everything!

Here is an example:
Word List:
1. Adjective: __BUMPY__ 2. Noun: __SOCKS__ 3. Number: __10,000__
4. Verb ending in "ing": __SINGING__ 5. Insect of choice __CRICKETS__

A __BUMPY__ bat ordered a big bowl of __SOCKS__
    1. adjective   *2. Noun*
ice cream with __10,000__ berries and __SINGING__ - __CRICKETS__ on it.
                3. number   *4. Verb ending in "ing"*   *5. insect of choice*

Prehistoric Halloween Fill-In Word List

1. Bug of choice _____
2. Adjective _____
3. Adjective _____
4. Favorite dinosaur _____
5. Number _____
6. Verb ending in "ing" _____
7. Type of insect _____
8. Something gross _____
9. Type of candy _____
10. Noun _____
11. Yucky noun _____
12. Something stinky _____
13. Marine reptile _____
14. Icky noun _____
15. Type of sweet _____
16. Type of insect _____
17. Type of ice cream _____
18. Yucky word _____
19. Type of pie _____
20. Least favorite dessert _____
21. Prehistoric Animal _____
22. Type of tree _____
23. Type of insect _____
24. Least favorite vegetable _____
25. Yucky dessert _____
26. Something disgusting _____
27. Animal _____
28. Number _____
29. Favorite candy _____
30. Adjective _____
31. Type of building _____
32. Number _____

The Prehistoric Halloween Buffet Menu

Welcome to the Prehistoric _____ Halloween Cafe where we serve the
                               1. Bug of choice

very _____ foods in town! All our food is prepared by world-renowned
        2. Adjective

chef _____ — _____ Le'Sweet. We have _____
       3. Adjective   *4. Favorite Dinosaur*   *5. Number*

Halloween dishes on our buffet table, including the chef's all-you-can-eat

specialty menu.

TODAY'S SPECIALS:

For starters, we have:

1. Ancient cheezy mozzerella _____ sticks.
                                  6. Verb ending in "ing"

2. Deliciously steamed _____ pot stickers.
                            7. Type of insect

For the main course, you can pick between:

3. The GARGANTUAN _____ — _____ burger on your
                      8. Something gross   *9. Type of candy*

choice of freshly baked sesame _____ buns, whole
                                10. Noun

grain _____ brioche, or organic sea salt _____ rye bread.
      11. Yucky noun   *12. Something stinky*

4. Aged _____ cheese Pizza, topped with your choice of
            13. Marine reptile

_____, and _____, or _____ and _____.
14. Icky noun   *15. Type of sweet* *16. Type of insect* *17. Type of ice cream*

Extra thin crust or double _____ stuffed crust pizza.
                            18. Yucky word

5. Stompingly delicious _____ spaghetti.
                             19. Type of pie

6. Deep fried seaweed and _____ tacos.
                                20. Your least favortie desert

For a lighter meal, we have two farm-fresh options:

7. Fresh _____ droppings noodle soup. With five roasted
             21. prehistoric animal

_____, on the side.
22. Type of tree

8. Jumbo _____, prehistoric _____ and
             23. Type of insect   *24. Least favorite vegetable*

_____ salad with extra _____.
25. Yucky desert   *26. Something disgusting*

For dessert, we offer a refrigerator-sized cup of _____ flavored
                                                  27. Animal

hot cocoa, accompanied by a _____ foot platter of _____.
                             28. Number   *29. Favorite candy*

And finally, a dinosaur sized slice of _____ prehistoric cherry pie
                                       30. Adjective

topped with _____ sized mound of whipped cream and
            31. Type of building

_____ blueberry bushes.
32. Number

Enjoy!

Quetzalcoatlus

Quetzalcoatlus (pronounced ket-sul-coo-a-tu-lus), found in North America, was the largest flying animal that we know of so far. They were just a little taller than the T-Rex (about the height of a giraffe). They were named after the Mayan and Aztec god, Quetzalcóatl, meaning "feathered serpent."

Halloween Story Game: Prehistoric Time Travel!

Finish the story however you like, and draw a picture to go with it!

You are on a long drive to a pumpkin patch. You start to doze off when you hear a loud sound that jostles you awake. As you look around, you are surrounded by a prehistoric world that you have only read about, or seen in movies. You quickly realize that you are no longer in your own time, or in a car, but on the back of a gigantic living...

_____

_____

_____

_____

Halloween Story Game: Prehistoric Time Travel!

You can continue your story here:

_____
_____
_____
_____
_____
_____
_____
_____
_____
_____
_____
_____
_____
_____
_____
_____
_____

Spinosaurus

Spinosaurus (pronounced: Spy-no-so-rus) was a gigantic 59-foot carnivorous **piscivore** (mainly fish-eating). In fact, **Spinosaurus** was one of the largest of all the theropod dinosaur fossils found so far, even larger than T-Rex! They have been found mostly in Africa. By the way, **theropods** are carnivorous (meat eaters) and most commonly **bipedal**, meaning they walk on two legs.
The use and reason for their giant crest are still mysteries. Some scientists think they may have been **semi-aquatic**, like hippos, living most of their lives in water.

Dinosaur Cave Art

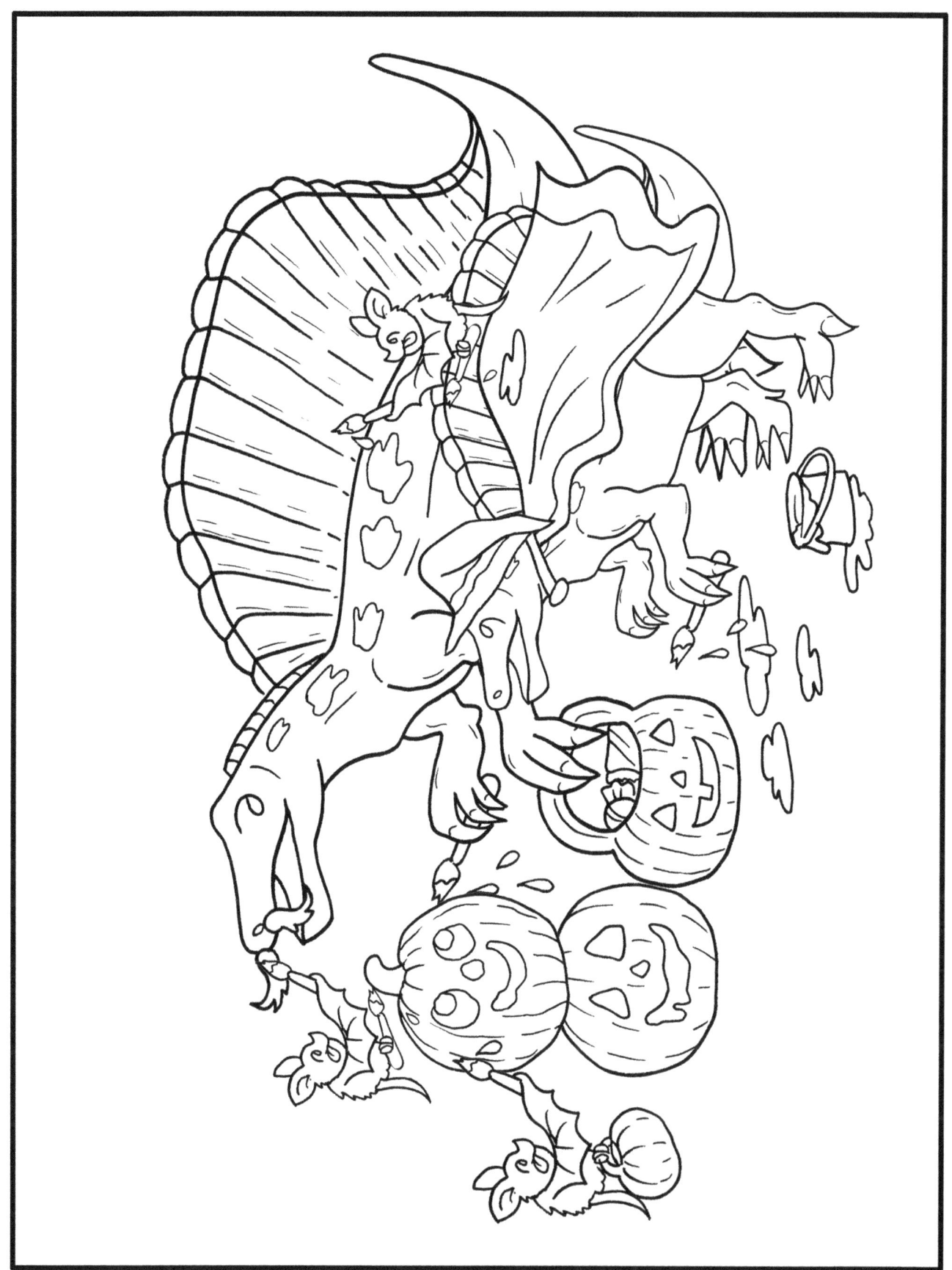

Draw a Halloween moon and help Spinosaurus paint a face on the prehistoric pumpkin.

Draw a funny face on the pumpkin.

Give your pumpkin a funny prehistoric name:

_____

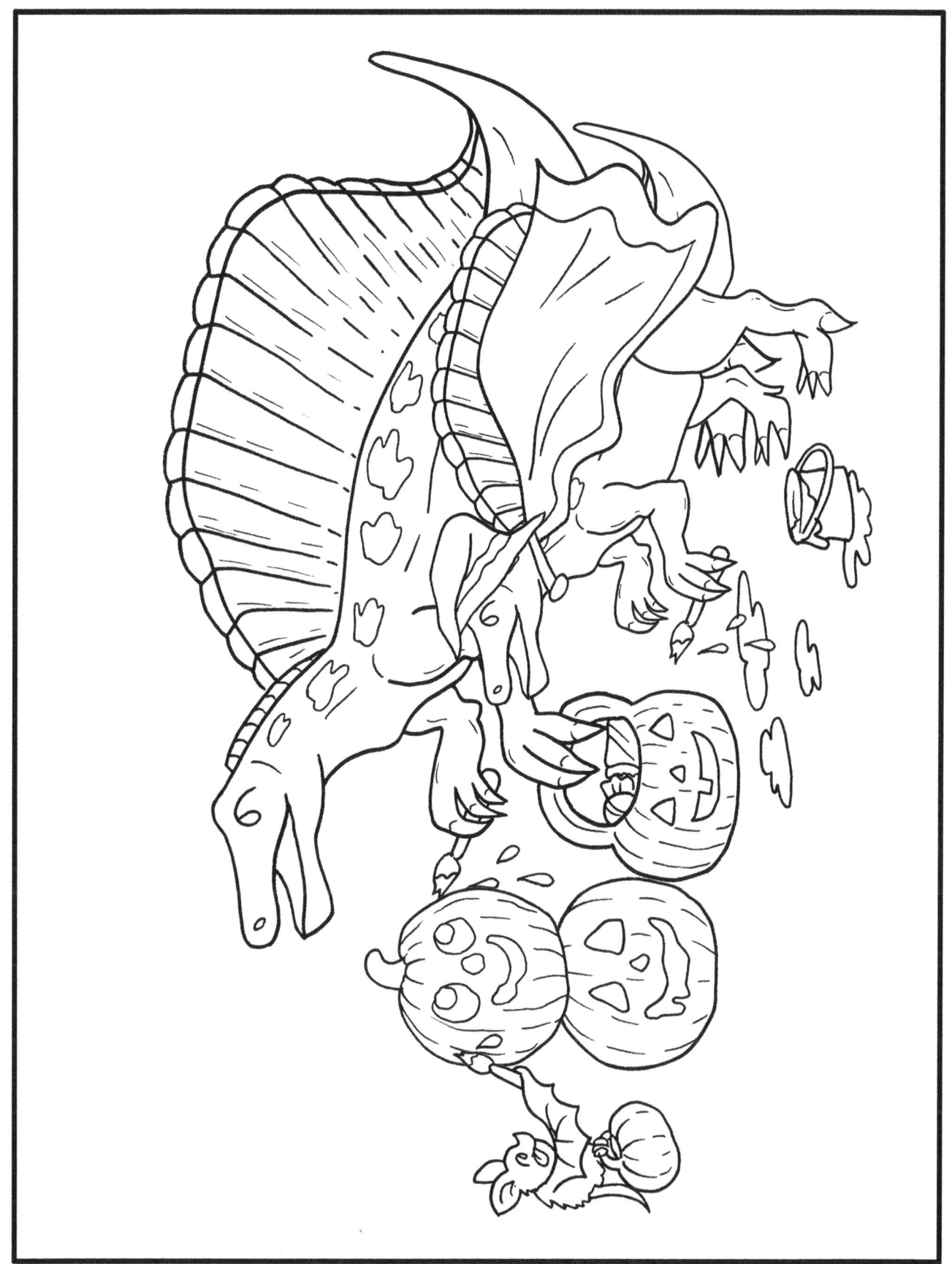

Shunosaurus

Shunosaurus (pronounced shoo-no-so-rus) was found in China and, so far, was the only **sauropod** (long-neck) found with a club on their tail. They were also one of the smaller sized sauropods.

Prehistoric Books and Movies

Write a list of your favorite dinosaur books and movies:

_____

_____

_____

_____

_____

_____

_____

_____

Magyarosaurus

Magyarosaurus (pronounced mag-ya-ro-so-rus) was the smallest **sauropod** (long-necked dinosaur) found so far, about as tall as a person when they were fully grown. They were discovered in Romania.

Happy Halloween

Let me tell you about my favorite dinosaur:

_____
_____
_____
_____
_____

Miragaia

Miragaia (pronounced meer-a-guy-a): What kind of dinosaur is it? Is it a sauropod (long neck)? Amazingly, no. This dinosaur belonged to the **stegosaur family**. **Mira** means "wonderful" in Latin, and the word **Gaia** comes from the name of a Greek goddess in charge of all life on Earth. Miragaia was about 21 feet in length meaning a little taller than a giraffe, or about the length of an Orca whale. They weighed roughly two tons, which was about the same weight of an adult white rhino at 4000 pounds.

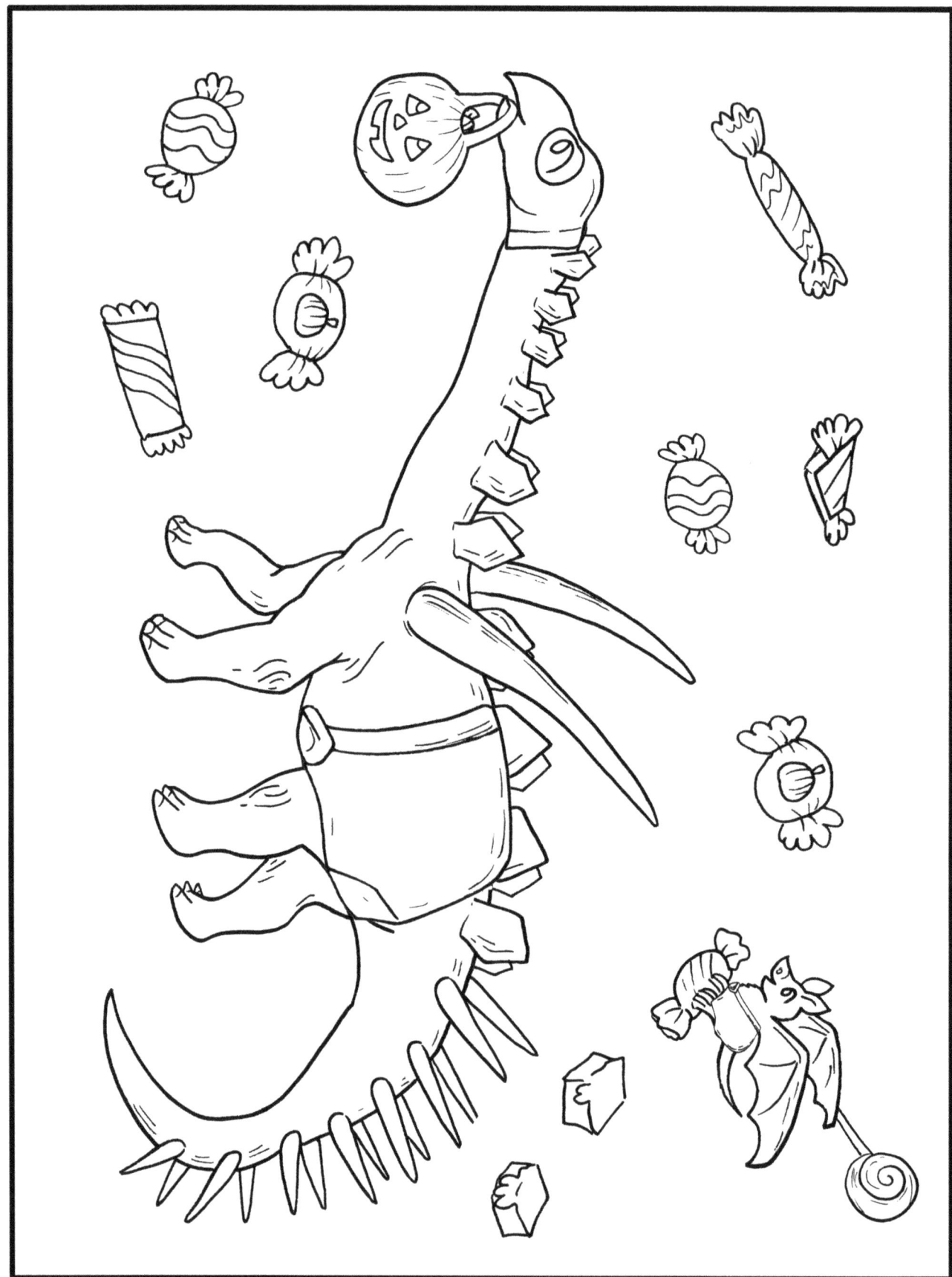

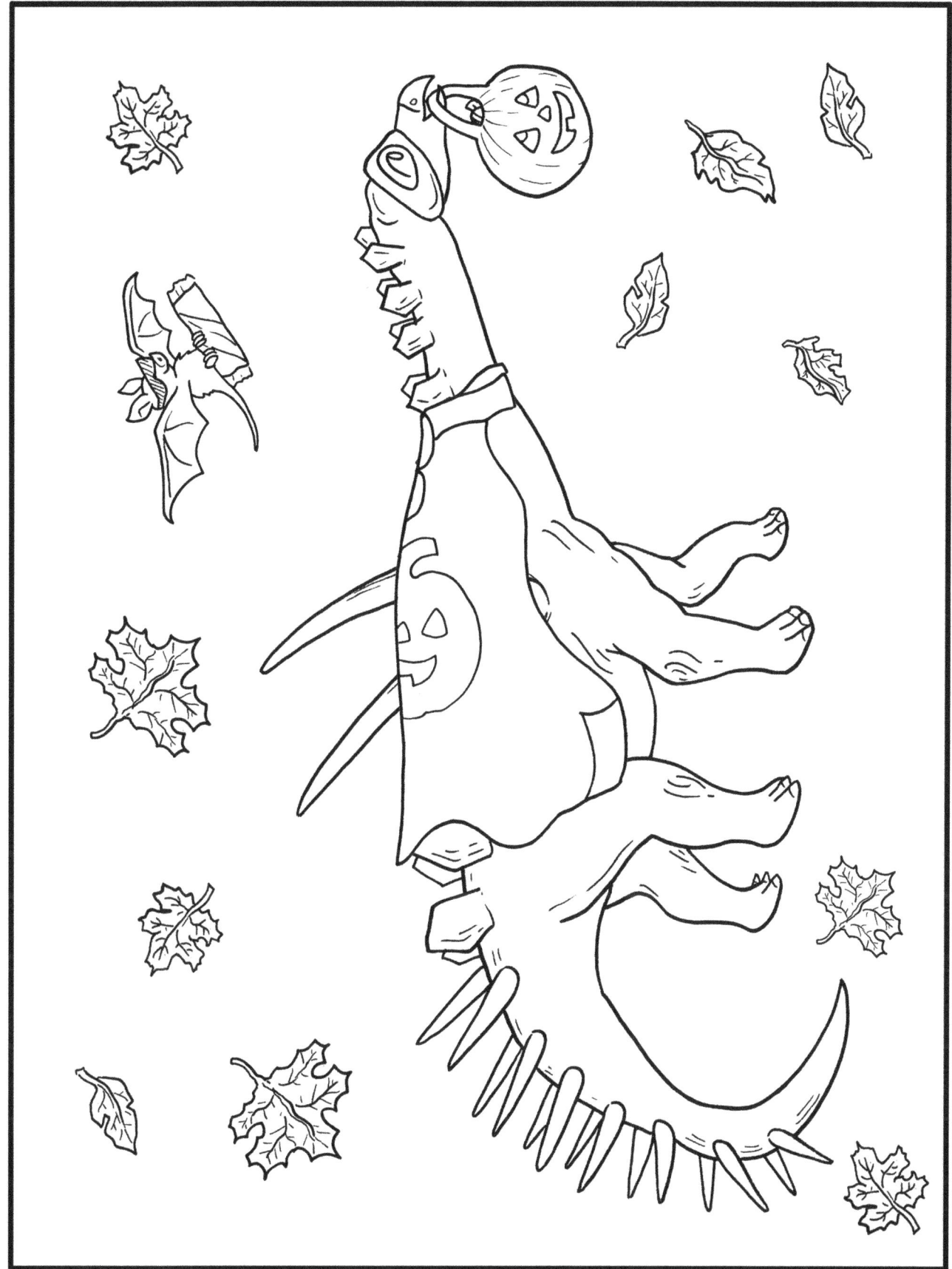

Miragaia Dinosaur Paper Doll

Instructions:

1. First **fully color** in the Miragaia Paper Doll and **all** six costumes.
*Make sure to **finish coloring before cutting**, or the pieces can rip.

2. Take out the paper doll and costume pages, **one at a time** and carefully cut them out.
*If it is too difficult, ask your parents or a grown-up to help you.
***Be extra careful not to cut off the tabs**. If you accidentally do, you can use tape to fix it.

3. Once all the pieces are colored in and cut out, fit the costume on the doll and fold back the tabs to help it stay in place. If you need help seeing how the costumes should look, just look at the **"Miragaia Paper Doll Examples"** on the next page.

*You can color and cut out the smaller **"Miragia Paper Doll Examples"** and **candies** if you want your own herd of Miragaia trick-or-treaters.

4. **Fully Color** and take out one, or all four, of the **"Trick or Treat house"** pages so you can take your Miragaia herd Trick-or-Treating from house to house!

5. You can save all the paper doll pieces in an **envelope or folder** when you are done playing. If you don't have an envelope, you can make your own by stapling or taping two pieces of paper together.

Most importantly, **have fun!**

Miragaia Paper Doll Examples

Here are the six Miragaia costumes. You can dress your doll like the examples shown here or mix and match them however you like.
Color and cut this herd out for extra fun.

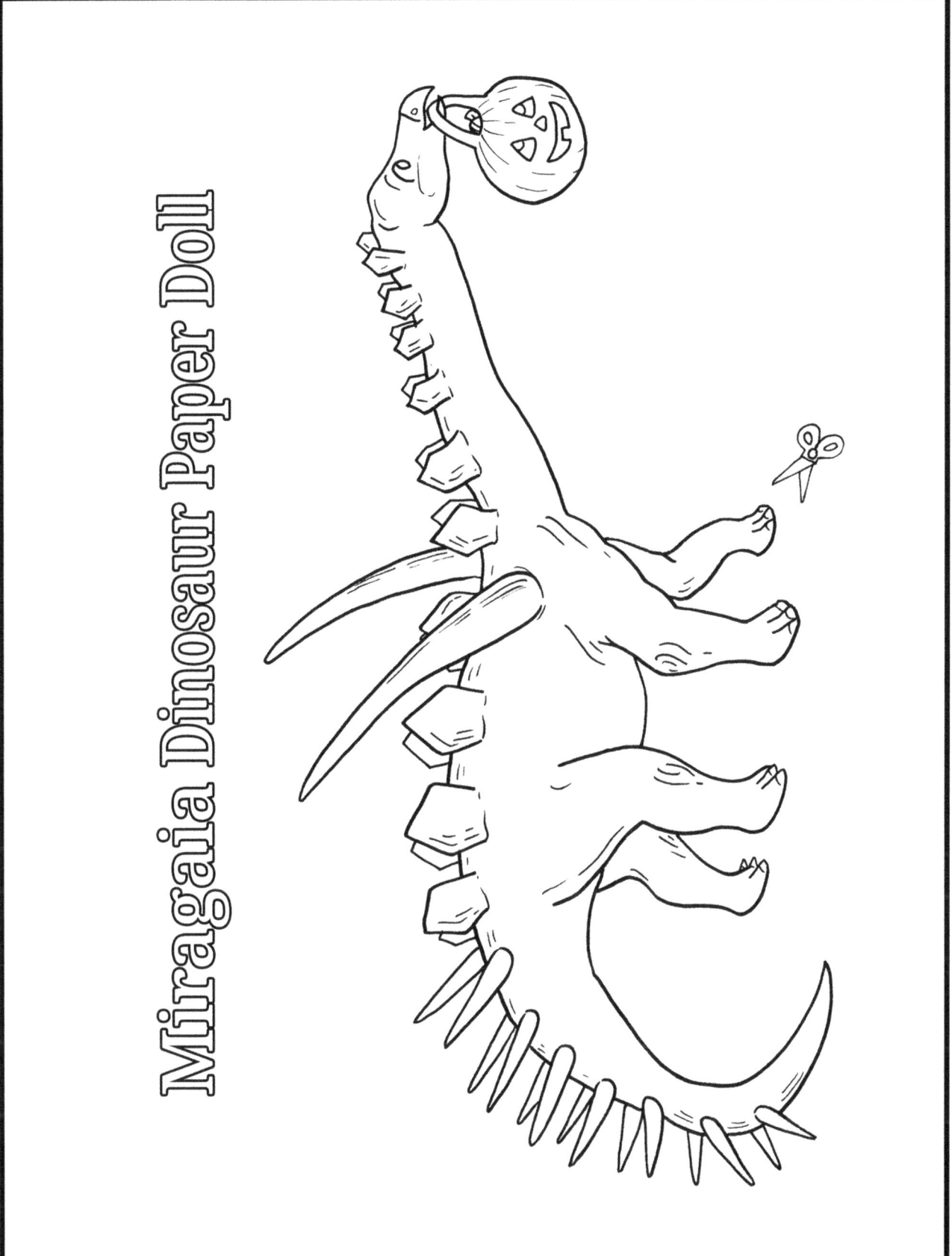

 # Miragaia Paper Doll Costumes 1-4

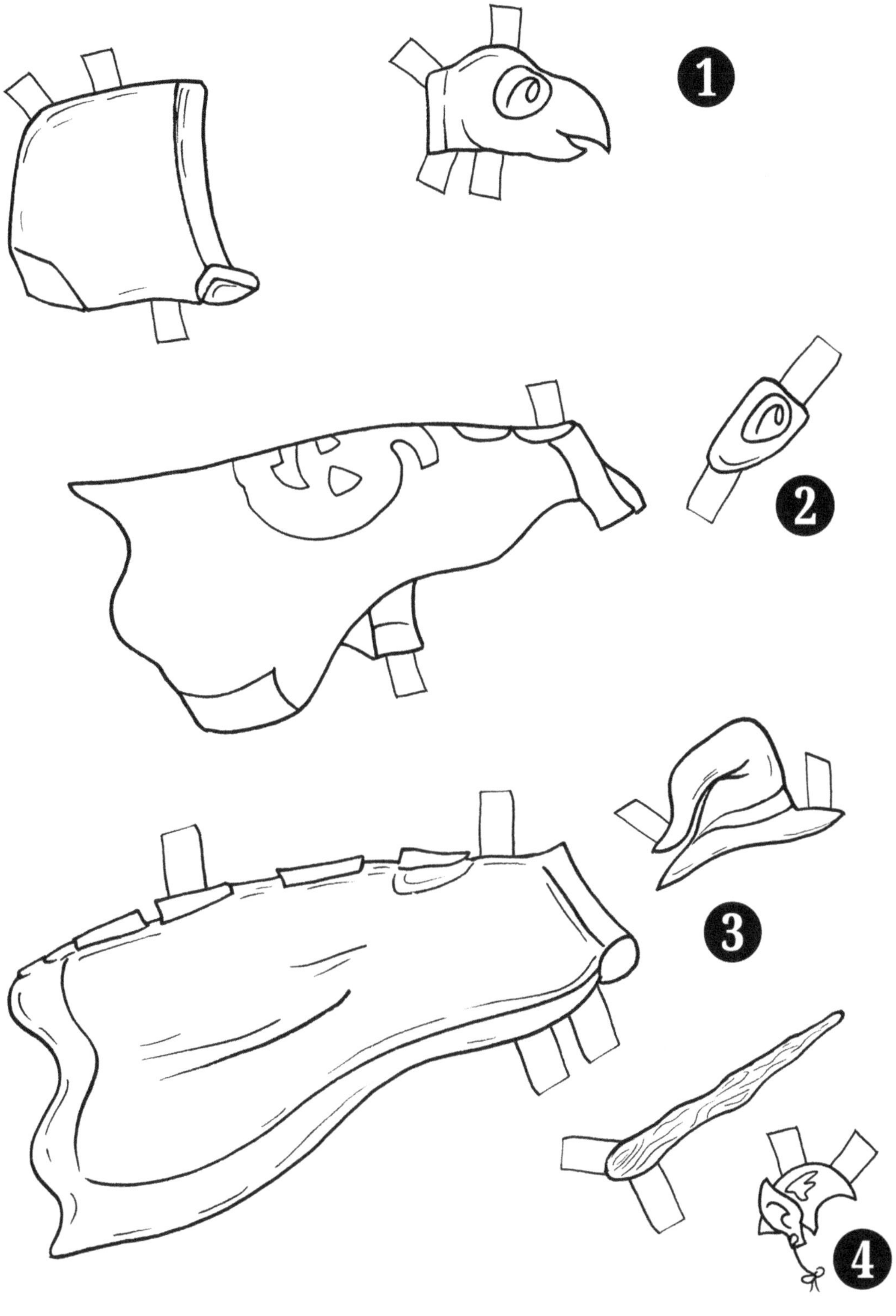

Miragaia Paper Doll Costumes 5-6

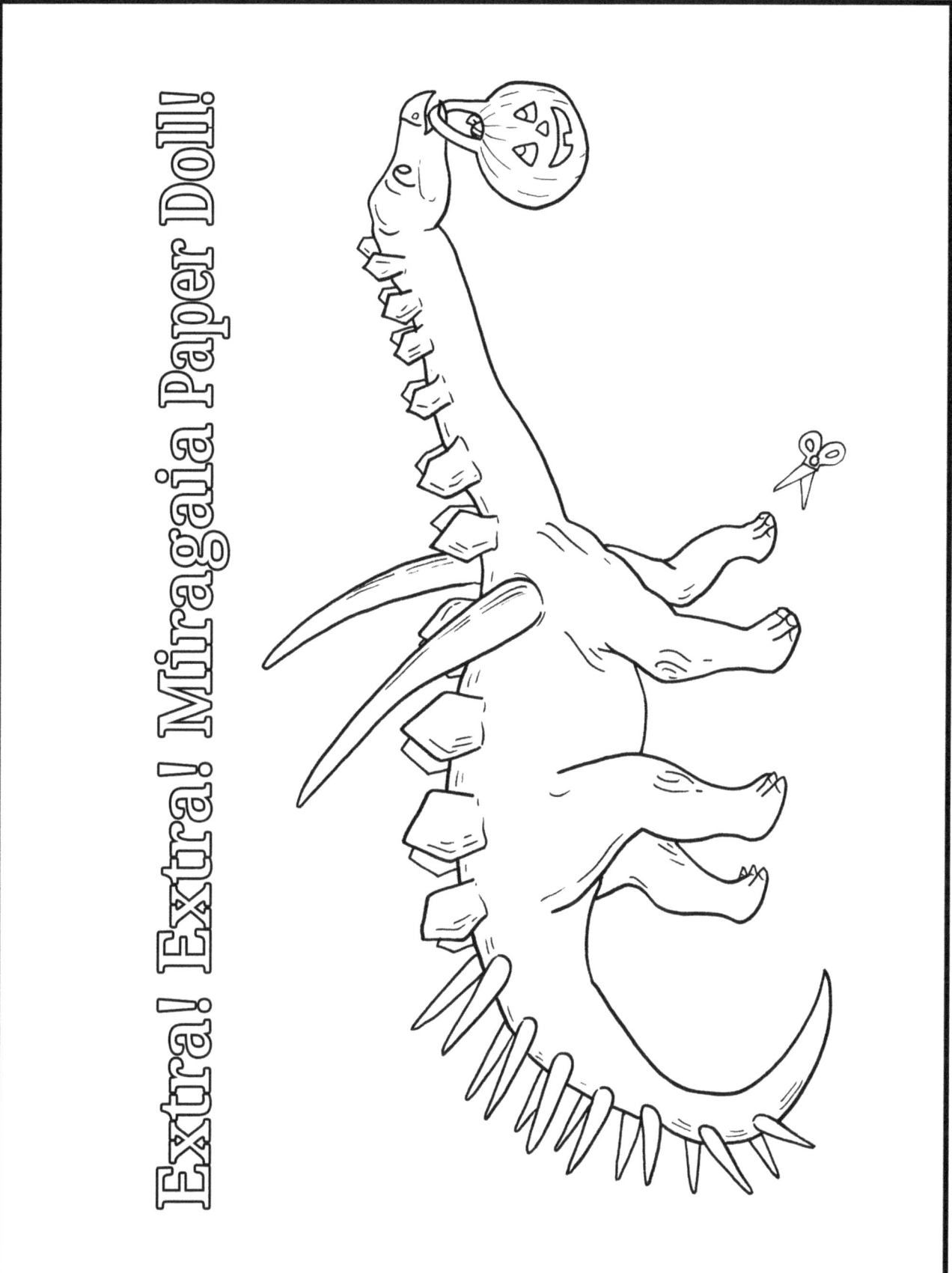

Halloween Neighborhood Playing Examples:

Once everything is colored in and cut out, take your dinosaurs trick-or-treating, then they can share their candies!

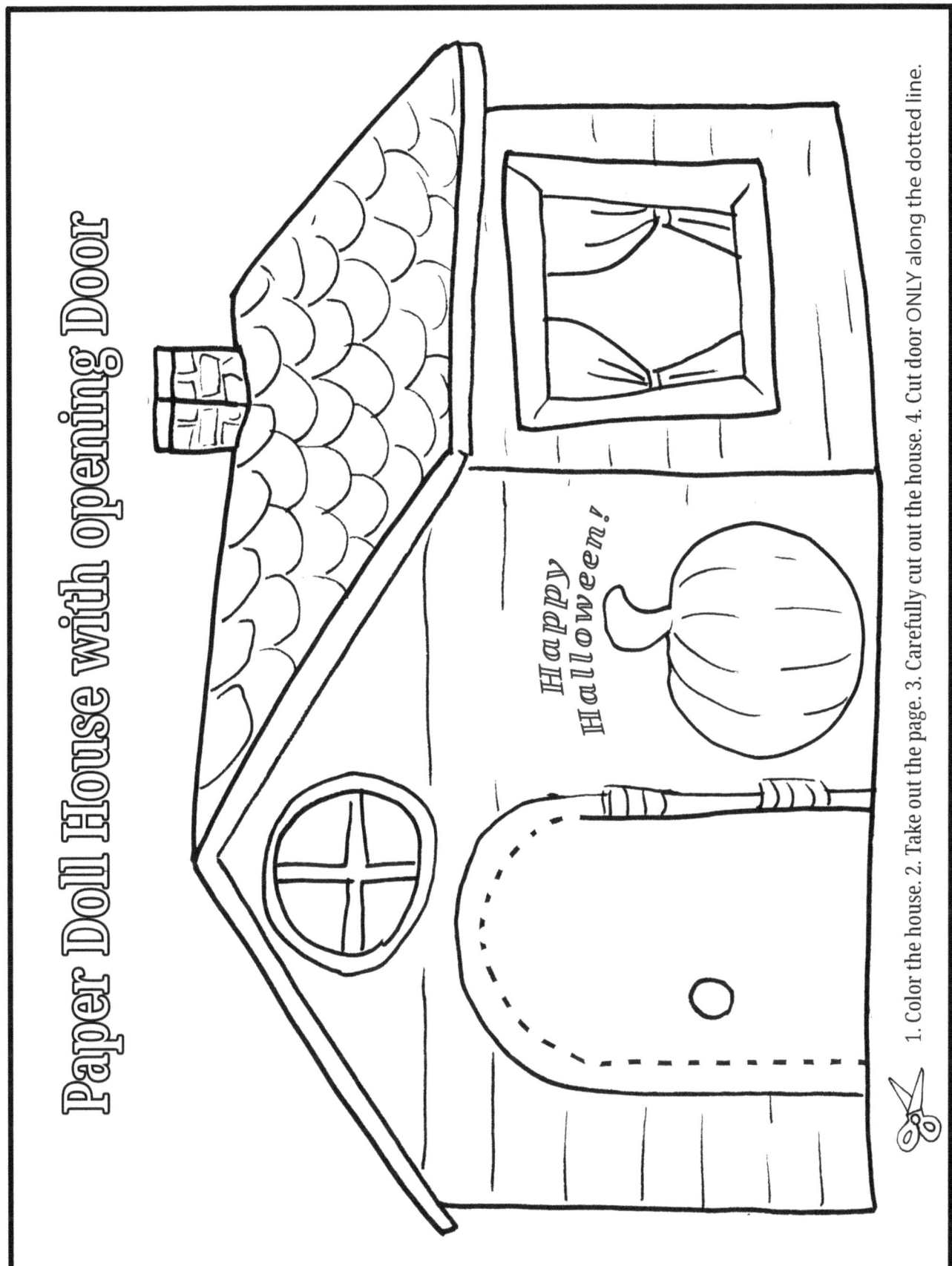

Paper Doll Trick-or-Treating Candy

Extra! Extra! Trick-or-Treating Candy!

www.ingramcontent.com/pod-product-compliance
Lightning Source LLC
Chambersburg PA
CBHW061352010526
44107CB00011B/909